DR. MARY T. JACOBS

Inspiring
Future
LEADERS
THROUGH COACHING AND MENTORING

Tandem Light Press 🐝

Tandem Light Press
950 Herrington Rd.
Suite C128
Lawrenceville, GA 30044

Tandem Light Press paperback edition February 2015

ISBN: 978-0-9854437-6-4
Library of Congress Control Number: 2014953089
Biblical passages are from the King James Bible
PRINTED IN THE UNITED STATES OF AMERICA

This book is dedicated to my husband, Rudy.

He has been my coach, mentor, and inspiration

for over forty wonderful years.

*If you have a goal and you do not act
upon it, then it is a shame!*

*If you have a talent and you do not develop it, then
it is a waste of what God has provided for you!*

*If you have a gift and you do not share the
gift, then you really do not have a gift!*

Please share your gifts, so we may all benefit!

CONTENTS

ACKNOWLEDGMENTS

I'd like to thank the following people for contributing to this book. Their insight and input was invaluable:

Mr. John Hagan, Mr. Tim Armstrong, Ms. Andria Bunner, Mr. Vic Verdi, Mrs. Cindy Antrim, Ms. Shennel Reedy. Special thanks to my colleagues and family for always believing in me and supporting me.

INTRODUCTION

WELCOME TO YOUR new journey. This book is intended to be used by educators, mentors, mentees, and others that may wish to learn how to give back to the world, in order to increase your giving and mentoring capacity; your gifts. As you begin to read and follow the lessons that I have learned and wish to share with you, please begin to think about your gifts. I believe in order for a "gift" to be a real gift it must be shared with others. The gift must be shared or given away to be a true gift.

I strongly believe we all have gifts to share, but first they must be recognized and refined. After many years of mentoring and coaching, I still wish to improve my skills as well as what I have learned along the way with others. Throughout my own mentoring and coaching journey, I always give my gifts, but I also receive many gifts in return from my mentees. And these are not physical gifts. The relationship and bond that I have made with my mentees has been powerful. I strongly believe that if all of us just gave back a little, we and our world would be so much better.

As you work through the exercises and reflection questions in this book, start thinking about the gifts that you have to offer others. These sections are included so that this book can act as a *living* workbook for you. Come back to it in a year, two years, five years, ten years, and see how your answers might be different.

Please list three gifts you currently have:

_____

_____

_____

List three important ideas you have learned from others:

_____

_____

_____

In the next chapters, we're going to take a look at lessons that I learned from coaches and mentors that I would now like to pass on to you. We'll also talk about how to help make you the most effective coach you can be. So don't be shy about filling in the responses and reflection areas. They are there to benefit you in the coming days, weeks, months, and years of your mentoring life.

Chapter 1

LEARNING AS A MENTEE

"A wise man learns by the experience of others.
An ordinary man learns by his own experience.
A fool learns by nobody's experience."

—Vern McLellan

S O MANY TIMES in life, we begin to reflect upon how and why we arrived where we are. There are folks along the way that help make us who we become. Thinking about these people and how they've shared their gifts with you is a powerful exercise. As we work through the book, we'll talk about how they fit into different categories and come at various times in our lives.

When I first started writing this book, I was hesitant to include too much of my own personal story. However, I soon realized that the reason I have the perspective I have on this topic is because of all of these amazing folks I've known and experiences I've had. Sharing them with you is my way of giving you some insight into how I arrived at a lot of the information here.

As a teacher for over twenty years prior to becoming an administrator, I had mentors that encouraged me along the way. In the beginning, the mentoring and guidance was more of what they thought about my skills and direction for my career. Some of these suggestions were all about the timing.

My First Real Job

During the Vietnam War, my husband was in the Air Force and had just returned from Guam. On his return we moved to North Carolina, and I found a job at Head Start. I was the Educational Assistant, and my job consisted of working with low-income families, supervising six different centers throughout the district, and working with students on the transition from Head Start to public school.

As I reflect back on this position, I realize how much I learned about others and myself. The director of the Head Start Association was Miss K. She was a retired, single principal that had dedicated her life to serving others, especially in the field of education. During our weekly staff meetings, I was often in awe of her knowledge and everything she had read. Each week we discussed our centers, and she always provided the leadership team with new reading materials as well as advice for what we were doing. But, I quickly realized the advice was not all about telling us what to do, but helping to guide us. I didn't recognize this at first, but as the year progressed this became evident to me.

One day, Miss K asked me to come and see her. My first

thought was, *Oh no*. I think that's a natural way to feel when your supervisor requests you to come and see them and it's not a scheduled meeting time. As I entered her office with my pad and pen, she sat behind her desk with a smile. She calmly asked me what I wanted to do as far as my career. As she let me think about my answer, she also said, "I know you have one more semester of student teaching in order to complete your degree from the University of Georgia." She waited for me to reply. I appreciate her letting me gather my thoughts before I answered.

I told her that my husband had been in Guam, and our family had not been together in over six months and student teaching had to be in a fifty-mile radius of the university. She quickly told me that was not always true. She told me about the potential I had for being a lifelong learner and leader. She pointed out the qualities that she had recognized in me. But, she told me, first I had to finish that degree. I couldn't move back to Georgia to finish my degree, I told her, due to my family. She told me that if I called the University of Georgia and was granted permission to student teach in North Carolina, she could find a professor from East Carolina University to supervise me. Well, after several phone calls to UGA I was granted permission. All I had to do was send UGA the tuition. I was thrilled!

Miss K allowed me to keep my job as I did my student teaching. After leaving my assigned school each day, I would return to my office and accomplish as much as possible. I remember being so grateful and thrilled about this opportunity. Miss K arranged for a professor to supervise me at the assigned school. He already had two other student teachers in the school. When I tell folks this story, they look at me like I was some type of brave rebel. That is not the case at all. I simply had a mentor that believed in me and made me **challenge the process**.

As I reflect back on what I learned from Miss K, the most important thing she did was believe in me! The other important thing I learned from her was to challenge the process. This had never occurred to me. I have taken these positive ideas and strive to use them with all of the people in my life: family, friends, and mentees.

REFLECTION:

Who do you believe in?

_____

What do you believe?

_____

What processes do you believe needs to be challenged?

_____

The journey continues for another twenty years! After living in North Carolina for about seven years, we moved back to Georgia. We moved to south Georgia where I met two outstanding leaders. They were my principal and assistant principal. Both of these leaders not only believed in me, but *trusted* me! They both gave me lots of responsibility at school and trusted that I would do my best. Both of them encouraged me to go into administration or be a counselor. When we had these conversations, I always told them that I had the best of both worlds. I had my class to teach, but had many opportunities for growth because they believed in me and trusted me. What more could anyone want? Not only did they believe in me and trust me, I did the same for them.

Reflection

Whom do you trust?

_____

_____

_____

Why do you trust them?

_____

_____

_____

Over the past thirty years, I have not been in contact with either of these mentors, but what they taught me has remained a part of me. Keep in mind as you continue to mentor, coach and develop your circle of friends that not all stay in the moment with you.

After living in south Georgia for seven years we moved to the Atlanta area. When I went to Gwinnett County to a teaching interview, I was blessed to have three interviews in one day. All three of the interviews were different, but there was one that I really wanted. During the interview process, one of the administrators offered me the position. *Wow!* What a great feeling. The next two interviews also yielded an offer, but not during the interview. Dr. W was my principal for the next several years. I can say it was wonderful! She guided me, gave me responsibility, and pushed me to do more. I use the word "push" because she thought of that as a growth opportunity. For example, when I had been teaching at my new position for about three months, she came into my room and said, "Well, you've been here about three months, and I think it is time to begin to take on more leadership opportunities."

I smiled and asked, "What do you have in mind?"

That was just the beginning. Before the year was over, I was on several committees county-wide. I was thrilled to be working with such an awesome person and mentor. We remained very close for years to come. She told me after I was named as an assistant principal to always do my best, and the next level would come. I have thought about that many times! I guess one of the best compliments she ever gave me was when she placed her son in my class and later asked me to loop up to the next grade and keep my class intact. During that period of time, the term "looping" was not fully developed. We just called it moving up!

Over the next two years, I got to know her even better since having her child in my room for two years. Not only did our relationship continue, but it remained until the day she passed away. To this day, I often think about what Dr. W would do. This was especially important when I later was named principal of a middle school. She died at an early age due to cancer. I guess God needed another mentor in heaven.

REFLECTION:

Who are the folks that push you?

_____

_____

_____

Whom do you push?

_____

_____

_____

Why are they worth the push?

_____

_____

_____

First Assistant Principal Assignment

After serving as a teacher in the district for six years, I finally decided that I wanted to apply for an assistant principal position. I interviewed for three different schools all in the same day. Are you seeing a pattern? All three of the schools appeared to have a different need. I determined this by listening to the questions and thinking about what they were really asking me. I was offered a position at the school that was my first choice. Again, I am so blessed!

It was the only position that I ever had an assistant principal partner. I now felt that I had two mentors that would shepherd and guide me. The assistant principal was a veteran of ten years and the principal had the reputation of being one of the best. They had different leadership styles, but provided lots of growth opportunity for me.

The principal gave me responsibilities and expected me to do them. I learned from her to always try to be student focused and do the right thing. As far as I know, every assistant principal she had later served as a principal or a central office director. That is powerful for any leader to develop so many people! We stay in touch, but not too often.

As far as the veteran assistant principal, we are joined for life! She is thoughtful in her actions and shines to this day as one of my mentors. She is also a dear friend. When I asked her something she always told me the truth and allowed me to think about the situation. She had a wonderful ability to allow me to develop **problem solving skills**; a skill needed by all leaders.

REFLECTION:

Name three powerful problem solvers.

_____

_____

_____

Why are they good problem solvers?

_____

_____

_____

My Days as the Principal

After moving to a small district and working as an assistant principal for one year, I applied for a principal position in the district. There were two openings; one at the middle school and one at the elementary level. During the interview process, I was asked to answer questions at both levels. The last interview was with the superintendent. He asked me which level I preferred. I told him elementary due to my experience at that level.

About an hour prior to the board meeting, the superintendent called and told me that he and the board members wanted me to go to the middle school and not the elementary school. Wow, have you ever had your mouth ready for vanilla ice cream, and then you get chocolate? He told me that it would be a **challenging** opportunity, but wanted my expertise in curriculum to be afforded to the middle school.

My seven years as the principal of the middle school were awesome. When I began, I planned to be there for about three years. However, when I arrived I realized that I loved the teenagers, and we had lots of work to do to move the school in the right direction. The superintendent was now my mentor and coach. During the first year, he asked me if I had ever thought about being a superintendent. And I had! He then told me to apply for the superintendent's training that would be about two years long. He said that the association would only take twenty-five candidates, and hopefully they would accept me as one of them, and they did! This was a growth opportunity that I loved! It is interesting that along the way, I discovered that I did not want to be a superintendent. I believe that growth opportunities and learning allows you to know yourself and what you really wish to do.

REFLECTION:

Describe a challenging opportunity you have had.

_____

_____

Who provided this opportunity for you?

_____

_____

_____

My Work at the University Level

I began my work with the university over ten years ago. On my goals list that I wrote during my student teaching, I said that one day I would be a college professor. So, when we were making a move after our children had graduated from college, I applied for a position at a college. After about three weeks, I was called to come in for an interview. We were still in the process of moving, so the timing was not the best. When I went for the interview, I had three parts to do. The first was to teach a class and be observed by students, as well as other faculty members. The second part was an interview with several professors. Last of all, interview with Dr. P. During that interview I was inspired by the way this professor spoke and her sincere concern for others. She was passionate about education, especially leadership.

When I left the interview, I reflected on the experience as I drove home. I was amazed how one person could touch and **inspire** me in just such a short time.

REFLECTION:

Please list two people that inspire you:

_____

_____

Why do they inspire you?

_____

_____

Throughout this book, we're going to look at ways to help you challenge the process, push yourself, problem solve, challenge yourself, and inspire others. I bet you'll be surprised at how much will translate into what you *teach* others.

CHAPTER 2
THE WHY OF MENTORING AND COACHING

❧

"Anyone who has ever been able to sustain good work has had at least one person, and often many, who have believed in him or her. We just don't get to be competent human beings without a lot of different investments from others."

— Life's Journey According to Mister Rogers

❧

MANY YEARS AGO, I heard someone say, "It is all about the dash in your life." I had to think really hard about that statement to realize that the day you are born until the day you leave the earth is the dash! I decided then and there that I would try my best to make my "dash" really mean something. For me, that dash is amplified with mentoring and coaching.

What does being a mentor or a coach mean to you? It means different things to different people! Is it something you need training to hone? Or are most people innately good at it? This workbook will help answer those questions so that you understand what being a mentor is, and the best way to get you there! Mentoring and coaching is part of my DNA, but is it yours?

In a few words describe what mentoring means to you:

_____

_____

In two years refer to what you wrote and then in five years. Has your description changed or has it stayed the same?

Now, describe what coaching means to you:

_____

_____

Do your answers seem similar? According to the Webster's Dictionary these words are very different:

Mentoring is a relationship between an experienced person and a less experienced person for the purpose of helping the one with less experience.

Coaching, when referring to getting coached by a professional coach, is a teaching, training or development process in which an individual gets support while learning.

Let's take a look if you have the skills in place to become an effective mentor. After you have answered and reflected on these questions, you will know if mentoring is right for you.

Ask yourself these questions:

Do you have the time or are you willing to devote the time needed to cultivate the relationship with a mentee?

_____

_____

Do you know why you personally should coach or mentor others?

_____

_____

Explain:

_____

_____

Do you have the power to see others potential when they do not see it?

_____

_____

Explain:

_____

_____

Do you have the ability to look past the present and to the future?

_____

_____

Explain:

_____

_____

Do you have the passion for developing others?

_____

_____

Explain:

_____

_____

Think about the person that has inspired you the most! Explain:

_____

_____

So far all of this sounds; like a walk in the park smelling the roses…Well, not always! There are times when things do not turn out the way you had in mind.

You're probably asking yourself: If this is time consuming and hard work at times, then *why* would anyone wish to do this? For me, there are several strong reasons that I WILL always be involved in mentoring and coaching. As you read my reasons, please determine if you share any of these attributes with me.

You may wish to write your own or comments underneath mine:

Mentoring and coaching brings me great joy!

_____

_____

_____

_____

Mentoring and coaching helps me grow and learn from others!

_____

_____

_____

_____

Mentoring and coaching has afforded me the opportunity to build lifelong relationships with others!

_____

_____

_____

_____

Mentoring and coaching keeps me involved with positive and motivated people!

_____

_____

_____

_____

If you agree with even two of the above reasons, then I believe that mentoring and coaching are what you need!

As you work with your mentees, you will have to understand that you are not the only force in their lives. This is an important concept to think about early on. They may be encountering others that are not so positive and encouraging. In fact, have you ever conducted a workshop and reviewed your evaluation and found lots of great comments and positive remarks, and all of a sudden read ONLY one comment that is not positive? It feels like a slap in the face! You, as a mentor, must develop that psychological hardness to stay positive and focused. My oldest brother used to say that is always easy to stay positive when everything is going your way, but it is a real test when it is not.

I've found that in order to stay positive and help my mentees stay positive, it's beneficial to have a few words that I say to myself when I need some encouragement. I read a quote by Jerry Rice some time ago that I developed into my own personal mantra that helps guide my thinking: "I will do and be today what others will not, so I can be and do tomorrow what others cannot do."

What is your personal mantra?

_____

_____

I made a conscious decision a long time ago that with God's help, I will define the person that I wish to be and wish to become! As you grow in your leadership journey, you will always have a few folks that wish to define your worth and destiny. So will your mentees. I encourage you to think about the following and share this list with them.

REFLECTION:

Are you willing to let one person define you?

_____

_____

_____

Why or why not?

_____

_____

_____

_____

What are the trigger words that bother you?

_____

_____

_____

_____

What can you do about these words?

_____

_____

_____

_____

You must realize that some things are out of your control, so let them go!

CHAPTER 3
BEING AN EFFECTIVE MENTOR

❧

"The roots of all our lives go very, very deep, and we can't really understand a person unless we have the chance of knowing who that person has been, and what that person has done and liked and suffered and believed."

— Life's Journey According to Mister Rogers

❧

PRIOR TO BECOMING a principal, I had the opportunity to serve as a mentor for an aspiring assistant principal. During this time, I was an assistant principal in a very large district—the largest in the state with over 150,000 students. When I asked the candidate about the requirements of the internship, she was a little vague. She simply said that she needed to get as much experience as possible. Not having any formal training in the proper ways to mentor, I resorted to what I knew.

The first step was to get to know the person. I call that just plain common sense. Later, I learned that not all coaches really embrace this notion, nor do they understand the importance of the relationship part of coaching. I later learned that common sense is not always common to everyone.

The second step was to introduce her to the good old file cabinet. Yes, I know, when you read that you will know that this happened quite some time ago. Of course, today all of these would be electronic files. We reviewed different documents she needed to develop for herself. I even invited her to make copies of any of my personal files. Again, I had no formal training for this role. I just called it sharing! These files included:

- How to Properly Conduct a Spelling Bee

- Interviewing

- Documenting an Employee

- Surveys for the Staff

- Open House Meetings

The list goes on and on. I know that as you review this, you may be thinking that these are very common to those of us in education. If you are observing, these topics appear to be simple, but when a person has to manage, develop, and lead the area, then it becomes far more important to detail and chronicle information. It may be that you are just observing and not leading the event.

Our third step was for my intern to observe me facilitating meetings and keeping a log. I asked her to reflect on what she observed and include lessons learned from each observation. She observed me conducting such meetings as:

- Special Education Meetings

- Meeting with Parents

- Meetings with Teachers

Her next step was to shadow me, then reflect on what she observed. This included the amount of time I actually spent on tasks during the day. My first experience as a mentor inspired me to want to continue and learn how to improve. I guess I did okay, especially because she was hired as the assistant principal when I left the district.

My next opportunity to mentor came when I was serving as a principal. During those seven years, I worked with different candidates from five universities. The requirements from each university ranged from A to Z. They had requirements from "do what *you* think the candidate should know" to a binder that was about two inches thick filled with too many requirements (busywork tasks).

All during these experiences, I was still learning and forming my own beliefs about mentoring and the life-long value it would hold for me. After joining Mercer University's Educational Leadership, I was asked to pilot the first yearlong performance-based internship department. This was the beginning of an adventure that has now turned into my passion.

YES, I was definitely hooked as a lifelong mentor. And I realized that mentoring was exactly what I was doing. I was more experienced than the teachers I was working with, but I was simply assisting them by giving them information and resources.

However, along the way, I moved my passion from mentoring to coaching.

Mentoring Vs. Coaching

There are three levels of mentoring. They include:

- Observing
- Participating
- Leading

All three of these forms of mentoring end in "ing." However, they are all very different in nature and depth of learning. The first type is *Observing*. Candidates must engage in observing. A trained coach will provide guidance as to the things and situations a person must observe. In other words, give some parameters. The guidelines I like to use are the ISLLC leadership standards.[1] Many scholars may disagree with some of these standards; however, they do provide the framework we may all incorporate into our work. You'll learn more about these standards in the next chapter.

---

1   http://illinoisschoolleader.org/documents/ISLLC_2008.pdf

Guidance for Observing

- Be specific in your notes while observing.

- Write down what you SEE, without added value…in other words, NOT your opinion.

- Correlate your observations to the standards.

- Which standards are you observing the most and the least?

- REFLECTION time with yourself is necessary as well as with your coach.

Lesson Learned

I still spend time observing leaders and leadership situations to determine styles, techniques and new skills. In order to continue growth, it is imperative to continue to develop your skills.

The second level of mentoring is *Participating.* In order for any of us to guide another person, we must learn to work in a group and be a participant. I do believe that in any situation we can learn from each other. Hopefully, these will be positive attributes, but there are times when a negative experience can be just as powerful! As you reflect on the participation of your experience, it is meaningful to determine what you learned from the experience as well as ways to improve the experience in the future.

"Reflection" is a keyword to being an effective leader! Reflection is not just thinking about something, but changing your mindset for the future. Reflection is defined as 1. the act of *reflecting* or the state of being *reflected*; 2. an image; representation;

counterpart; 3. a fixing of the thoughts on something; careful consideration.

GUIDANCE FOR PARTICIPATING

- Be specific about understanding your roles and responsibilities in the group.

- Ask specific questions for clarity.

- Continue to observe and watch others in the groups to determine style and the way they proceed with his/her work and responsibility.

- At this level, it is important to know as much as possible about your styles of leadership and how you might adapt your styles to foster a greater participation in the group.

- Continue to use a variety of instruments such as 360 and leadership inventories to gain information about your characteristics and style.

- If your style is predominately one area, then seek to enhance the other styles of leadership.

LESSON LEARNED

Knowing your leadership style and practicing in a group will help prepare you for the next level, which is LEADING. During this stage of internship, PARTICIPATION is also in place to make sure you are a TEAM player.

The last, but certainly not the least of the levels of mentoring, is *Leading*. It is amazing when you move from **observing** to **participating** to **leading** how quickly your stress level may grow. It is somewhat like being at a ballgame and yelling to the team on the field how to play the game, but then you are given the ball and bat and asked to lead.

Think of a time when you were asked to lead a professional project or initiate one. Can you remember how you felt? What were you thinking? Were you excited or a little bit frightened? It could have been all of these feelings. Take some time to reflect on how you felt.

_____

_____

_____

_____

The greatest difference in mentoring and coaching is that mentoring is the relationship between an experienced person and a person with less experience, typically in a professional capacity.

Mentoring is:

- Actively listening
- Building a relationship between you and your mentee
- Offering advice
- Offering care and concern

Coaching is:

- Teaching a mentee, so they build capacity
- Training a mentee, so they build capacity and begin to acquire skills to help others
- Developing the mentee to problem solve and process
- Providing specific information, but not telling them what to do
- Capacity is the KEYword!

CHAPTER 4
STANDARDS AND GUIDELINES

❧

"Let us raise a standard to which the wise and honest
can repair; the rest is in the hands of God.

— George Washington

❧

I N THE WORLD in which we live, standards and guidelines offer us the guidance and criteria to ensure that we all offer the best quality of services. If you think about this, some of us will have different opinions. Consider this: Should we NOT have standards for the medications we take or the foods we eat? Think about your opinion. Exactly. We have to have standards to ensure consistency and quality. Mentoring and coaching are no different.

When coaching leadership candidates, a system of requirements needs to be addressed. Reviewing the standards and determining the needs of the candidate is critical. The ultimate goal is for the candidate to go to the next interview, and when asked, "What is an area of weakness you have," the candidate can reply, "once it was_____, but due to an intense internship and coaching, this is how this was corrected."

Regular meetings and time spent with a candidate are a must. They need to be systematically scheduled. Group meetings with other interns are powerful. Remember, the goal is to build capacity for the candidate when you have limited contact, for the person to reflect on lessons learned and be able to make decisions and move the organization forward.

In the last few years, I have been analyzing the types of goals candidates selected and determining if there is a pattern as I correlate them to the standards. So far, it is balanced! We will see as time progresses.

In the last chapter, I shared with you that I prefer to use the ISLLC standards. There are six standards, but I have added Performance Based Internship. I feel that as the mentee is observing and participating they must be provided with specific guidance for each standard.

Standard 1: Setting a widely shared vision for learning.

Suggestions for this standard:

- Analyze the school's vision and mission statement. How was it developed? Who was involved? When was it revised? Should it be revised? How is it shared?

- Review several other vision statements from other districts. Compare and contrast.

- Review board policies.

- How is data used in the system and shared? Who is responsible?

- Observe meetings and note how decisions are made.

Standard 2: Developing a school culture and instructional program conducive to student learning and staff professional growth.

Suggestions for this standard:

- Review how student schedules are developed to make the best use of instruction time.

- Review the current curriculum and determine how it is implemented and monitored.

- How is professional learning developed, delivered and monitored?

- How and when are students tested and information shared?

- How is school safety ensured and monitored?

- Is action research used to help inform decisions in the school?

Standard 3: Ensuring effective management of the organization, operation, and resources for a safe, efficient, and effective learning environment.

Suggestions for this standard:

- Review system's policies and procedures as well as the school's procedures. What are your findings? What changes should be made?

- Explore the use of technology. Is this meeting the needs of the 21st century learner?

- Interview different services in the district to gain an understanding of how it is managed; such as: food service director, resource officers, maintenance director, etc.

- Interview random groups to determine the perception of the school and or district, such as: extra-curricular activities, students, parents, community members.

Standard 4: Collaborating with faculty and community members, responding to diverse community interests and needs, and mobilizing community resources.

Suggestions for this standard:

- How is the curriculum monitored for all students? Who is in charge of this? Describe any issues needed and how the steps for improvement are developed.

- Interview different leaders and determine how parent involvement is handled, maintained, and improved.

- How is culture in the school developed and enhanced for all students?

- Explore the resources that are available at the school. How is it communicated with the community?

- Describe how volunteers and partners are developed for the school and or system. Write a report for improvement.

Standard 5: Acting with integrity, fairness, and in an ethical manner.

Suggestions for this standard:

- Review job descriptions for leaders, teachers, and other school personnel. Analyze the forms of evaluation and reflect on the alignment of the description and the evaluations.

- Observe how leaders act with integrity and fairness. Reflect upon what you observed.

- Develop questions and interview stakeholders with regards to fairness and integrity of teachers and leaders in the school. Write a reflection on your findings.

Standard 6: Understanding, responding to, and influencing the political, social, legal, and cultural contexts.

Suggestions for this standard:

- Review school board training for your district.

- Observe school board meetings in several districts and write a reflection on your findings.

- Develop a system to be informed about local, state, and federal changes in education.

- Interview the school board attorney, local judges, and Human Resource director to gain insight into legal aspects of the job.

- Attend tribunals and court hearing for students.

- Maintain and update legal training (i.e., Harben and Hartley and Associates).

Standard 7: Performance Based Internship

Mentee develops a yearlong project and leads!

Examples of some of the projects:

- Leading the system through SACS accreditation

- Leading the system through new lines of dividing the county and or system.

- Developing a discipline handbook and leading the school through the implementation of appropriate discipline.

- Leading and developing the new teachers yearlong professional learning plan and support.

- Developing and leading changes in curriculum to afford a better learning environment.

- Leading the math adoption and developing appropriate technology to support the new math adoption.

- Leading the implementation of the new curriculum (i.e., Common Core).

As I guide my mentees, I provide specific directions. I have them refer to the standards, assess needs, and celebrate accomplishments as we continue our journey. I encourage you to do the same, both with your own successes and your future mentees.

CHAPTER 5

GUIDANCE AND TRAINING FOR COACHES AND INTERNS

===

ॐ

"We're here for a reason. I believe a
bit of the reason is to throw
little torches out to lead people through the dark."

— Whoopi Goldberg

ॐ

THE QUOTE ABOVE by Whoopi is powerful to me because it is true that we must be passionate about why we wish to do certain things, why we're setting goals we're setting, and the legacy we want to leave. So, the first key to the guidance and training for coaches is that the coach must be passionate about the work. As I have mentioned earlier in the book, this is my passion.

Intentional Communication

We talked in Chapter 1 about the need to stay positive and keep a positive outlook when communicating with your mentees. Intentional communication is very important when working with someone professionally. Think before you speak and act, and be sure you are giving them the best, most accurate information you have available to you. Don't be afraid to ask your own mentor, or seek outside assistance if you are struggling with how to help.

Obviously since you're reading and participating in this workbook, you're on your way to learning more about the process of mentoring and coaching. There are different levels of coaching that can be learned. First of all, as you coach an individual, you must get to know the person. Relationships are vital for having trust. You have often heard that folks don't want to know what you know until they know you care. True, very true!

Something I heard once was, you manage by sending e-mails, and you lead and connect by face-to-face conversations. Too many times we send e-mails and text messages when we should be picking up the phone and calling or going to see a person. We have lost so much of our integral meaning and conversations by e-mailing and texting that it causes me even to be more conscious about calling others. If you wish to send a short and sweet e-mail or text that is fine, but writing details that may be misunderstood is wrong. It reminds me of the third-grade behavior on the playground, when one child hits another and runs away. Not the way to connect with another person and certainly not the way to settle any disagreement.

Human Interaction

How many times have you driven through an old town and noticed the wraparound porches on the front of the houses? When I was growing up, my mom and dad sat on the porch most every night and talked. Dad would sometimes smoke his pipe. He told me it was to keep the bugs away. What a peaceful thought! Most of the houses in the early years had porches, and I remember always having family and friends to come for Sunday dinner after church. It was also just fine to stop by for a quick visit without calling to see if it was okay. Then something changed. We began building back porches with decks that could not even be seen from the front of the house. Sometimes we said this was for privacy. Perhaps it was for privacy, but could it be the first signal to tell others not to enter your space. You think about it. In your life, what are the porches that you have built? Where are they located?

I challenge you the next time you take a ride through a small town, notice what you see.

REFLECTION:

What did you discover?

_____

_____

The four-way stop sign:

How many of you don't mind stopping at the four-way stop sign. I don't! Sometimes I get amused when I come to one and watch the other cars. We all know the rules or should know the rules about taking turns at the "four-way stop sign," but I love to watch the look on the motorists' faces as they wait their turn. Some motion for you to go first, when clearly it is not your turn, others have a glare on their face that makes you believe they are about to run you over.

Think about the next time you come to a four-way stop sign and what are you thinking. I always think after watching the folks, *wouldn't it be great if we took turns and were considerate of others?*

REFLECTION:

Describe your typical behavior at the four-way stop sign.

_____

_____

_____

_____

Describe what you observe others doing.

_____

_____

_____

_____

Other guidelines and resources for mentoring:

* Reading and gathering information about Race to the Top guidelines[2] (which clearly state the need for support for principals as well as teachers) will help you understand the urgency for coaches.

---

2 http://www2.ed.gov/programs/racetothetop-assessment/index.html

- Learning how to listen and clarify prior to giving feedback is another key component. We often are trying to answer, prior to a person even finishing their questions. I have learned that educators are probably more guilty of this than professionals in any other field. This is not to criticize educators, but it is part of the work done on a daily basis. Listen more than you speak.

- Learn how to map out the outcomes for a period of time (specifically, a yearlong plan is best). I stress a 90-day action plan in some cases, but for real systemic changes, a year is needed. Coaches will need to assess what a candidate will need. Sometimes this will take several different measures to determine and pinpoint how to proceed. In performance coaching, we use different instruments. The first is the use of the ISLLC standards, which guide the majority of the work.

- There are many different institutions that offer coaching classes and certifications (see Resources in the back of the book). You may do a search for some near you, but I always like to rely on what my peers share with me prior to going to another class. Even if you have coached candidates for years, it is imperative that you continue to attend and learn the newest and best practices.

Performance Based Internships

Some states require a performance based certification for their leaders. Universities were *required* to develop a program for principals. This initiative began several years ago, and the growing need and appreciation for the endeavor has been extremely favorable! Currently, not all principals hold a performance based certification; however, if my crystal ball is correct, I do believe there will be a push to encourage all principals to achieve this certification. Some districts have considered this requirement for leaders. As they begin to renew their certificates, they are encouraged—or will be required—to earn the performance based certificate. In fact, the performance based certification is a win-win for all stakeholders. The principal candidate earns the certification and increases their capacity to lead, while the district is afforded a trained performance coach who will work with the candidate for a minimum of one year. During that yearlong internship, the performance coach, along with a school or system-based mentor/coach, works with them and provides guidance. A team of at least three is involved in determining the needs and goals the candidate must set with respect to the standards.

Along with the ISLLC standards, districts and universities align their roles and responsibilities and other standards as well as the district goals to ensure that all the dots are connected. The goals must be something that will benefit the school and or district, as well as the individual.

CHAPTER 6
REAL STORIES
FROM MENTEES

ھ

"Obstacles don't have to stop you.
If you run into a wall, don't turn around and give up.
Figure out how to climb it, go through
it, or work around it."

— Michael Jordan

ھ

JOHN HAGAN

John Hagan was a Physical Education teacher during the internship
experience, but now serves as an alternative school principal. Please
note his journey of leadership!

My leadership vision began the first year I began teaching
back in 2005. Note, I finished my Masters of Education and

wanted to obtain my leadership certification. However, all the leadership certification programs I looked at required leadership candidates to have a minimum of three years teaching experience. Thus, I had to teach a couple more years to meet these criteria. Unfortunately, this hurdle was just the beginning of my challenges to become an administrator. These challenges ranged from the state making leadership certification changes to system-level politics. I will now detail these leadership chronicles.

State Changes Leadership Criteria

In 2007, the state of Georgia began an initiative to change all the leadership certification criteria. One of the main changes was the admission process for leadership candidates being accepted into leadership preparatory programs. The main changes were that leadership candidates already had to be serving in leadership positions, along with the requirement that local superintendents must sign off on leadership preparatory program paperwork. All these changes required leadership candidates to go through several obstacles. These obstacles became a huge barrier to me because I was working in a very rural and small school system. Meaning, I was not a native of the county where I worked. Consequently, the odds of getting my superintendent to sign off on my leadership paperwork were highly unlikely. Additionally, I did not have a leadership position! Nevertheless, I was still faithful and committed to my vision of becoming an administrator.

My First Attempt

In 2008, I was ready to initiate the process of becoming an administrator. Further, I was accepted into a local university's leadership program. And, I had completed all the requirements except for one! This requirement was the local superintendent's acknowledgment that I served in a leadership position or the paperwork as described above. So, I went to my principal and asked her to sign off on the paperwork, but she was reluctant to do so. I then went to the superintendent, but he would not sign off on the paperwork. He stated that I did not serve in a leadership position, and there were no leadership positions available. In other words, he was not going to sign my paperwork! So, my dream to become an administrator was shot down! I was a little bitter in the way they handled my request. But, I shook it off and did not let it get the best of me. I prayed long and hard about this challenge. And, I discerned the true lesson of how God answers your prayers. He answers them with "Yes," "No," and "Be Patient!" I really felt this Godly lesson was not the answer of "No" but rather "Be Patient!" In other words, be patient and wait for the right time for this blessing to reveal itself.

My Second Attempt

My second attempt came when I heard that Mercer was starting a leadership program in Savannah in the fall of 2009. I researched the program and was very impressed! I sent my admission application in and was accepted into the program. Fall was fast approaching, and I was ready to start the program. But, at the last minute, the program was put on hold because there were not enough students enrolled in the program. Again, I knew that it was God working! I was closer to reaching my goal, so I remained positive. This positive mindset is what fueled me even more to become an administrator. Again, I owe God for this blessing! It was this adversity that made my mind stronger and my will more powerful. Again, I discerned that God was teaching me how to be a patient leader. I learned that these traits are mandatory if you are going to be a strong leader in any context. This lesson taught me the true meaning of patience being a virtue.

My Third Attempt

The third attempt came one afternoon in the fall of 2011. I was very tired of my chaotic work environment and needed a change. I had Mercer's phone number still programmed in my phone, so I called them. No one answered at first, so I was transferred to another extension. This nice lady answered the phone, and it happened to be an angel (she knows who she is). I spoke to her and told her that I was ready to drive to Macon to complete Mercer's leadership program. She responded by asking if I had submitted my admission paperwork. I responded back by saying, "Yes, back in 2009, and I was already admitted into the program!" She then said they were starting a leadership program in Savannah in the coming winter. I knew it was meant to be this time. In January 2011, I started Mercer's leadership program.

I Was Not Locally Born and Raised

My local school system is full of politics, but all things have some politics. And, unfortunately, I was not a native of the county where I worked. This issue compounded my leadership certification journey greatly. However, I still had faith and patience it was all going to be okay. To add, I was enjoying Mercer's program. Simply, I really enjoyed learning about leadership. I had never felt such passion for learning, but this time, I did. This passion was my drive to keep going; or, it was

God's way of motivating me to keep my faith strong and patient. Time passed, and again the challenge of getting my leadership paperwork signed by the superintendent surfaced. Then, there was this one Mercer professor who saw my leadership potential. She had faith in my abilities to become a strong leader. Further, she called my superintendent and explained the leadership certification process to him. He was unaware of a few things! She also asked him to sign off on my leadership certification paperwork; and, like Moses and the Red Sea, the waters parted for me! Meaning, my superintendent signed off on the paperwork and let me complete my leadership internship. But, this was not the only blessing; they also offered me an administrator's position at the end of my internship. I am now serving as director of this system's alternative school!

LESSON LEARNED

John's story is filled with goal setting and perseverance. He possessed an inert ability to understand this notion; therefore, I have no doubt he will continue his leadership journey for many years to come.

TIM ARMSTRONG

Tim Armstrong is a high school teacher in Oconee County, Georgia. He reflects and describes his performance-based internship and experiences. As you read, please pay close attention to his goals being related to his specific needs, as well as the needs of the school. In other words ... meaningful work!

Tim began his work in the summer. He had the opportunity to work with the leadership team. The summer experience is all about observing and participating. The principal appeared to be an outstanding planner. I have discovered that many times this is a weakness. Taking the time to **assess and plan** is priceless. When the task becomes difficult, it is imperative to have a solid plan based on planning and data.

Tim stated he felt the summer internship was powerful! He designed schedules and opportunities for the students throughout the year. One of the reflections he shared was taking the time to plan and explain to the teachers about the changes and having them be a part of the decision-making.

In Tim's words:

One of the many things I've learned in my time at Mercer is that you have to **promote the good things** that are happening at your school. One of the newspapers I contacted ran an ad for me in the paper to help advertise, and one even sent a reporter to interview me and writeup an article in their paper.

One of the biggest things I have learned is how to **balance taking instructional time** away from teachers vs. taking time for a guest speaker. I've sat down with my principal and talked for weeks. Another thing I've learned this year is how to see the big picture, how the school schedule has many more parts that must be **blended** together.

During this internship, I learned how to allow **teachers and other staff members to give input.** We started talking about the registration process in October. As the Science Department chair, I had to meet with the Assistant Principal for Curriculum and the Principal to discuss course offerings for the upcoming year. When it came time to discuss the registration process, the Assistant Principal came up with a plan for meeting with all of the students during homeroom by grade level in February, then meeting in homeroom the next week for "**roll back.**" Roll back is our process of having students go back and visit their teachers from the fall semester to get signatures for classes for the next year. Registration is a process that we must go through, and I think that our Assistant Principal for Instruction did a great job allowing people to voice their opinion on the process and how to best work through it.

As a future administrator, I think the most important thing I can do is **communicate** with teachers and staff members. During a process like registration, teachers and staff members are going to be required to put in extra hours and make recommendations for students. By communicating throughout the process, teachers and staff members feel like they have the ability to provide feedback. They are going to be much happier when fulfilling their duties.

I've also learned to **lean on various experts** within the school and the system. Early on in your administrative tenure, I think you feel more of the need to do everything yourself and micromanage so that everything is perfect. While this sounds great on the surface, it is impossible to do, and it will drive your staff crazy. I think one of the more important things you must do as an administrator early on is to learn whom you can trust and what you can trust them with. If you continue to micromanage, you will run yourself ragged, but you will also not produce the best product or allow those around you to grow.

I've been a teacher for thirteen years, and a couple years ago I began to feel like I had seen enough and experienced enough in the classroom where I would not be surprised as an administrator, and also that I had something to offer to other teachers.

This internship specifically has given me lots of practice and experience **leading** a group of people, learning to **communicate** with the whole group, building relationships, and empowering the teachers to be **involved**—in other words, **building capacity in others!**

In conclusion, Tim's work and leadership focused on the needs of the school.

SHENNEL REEDY

Shennel Reedy is currently an assistant principal in a high school in Savannah, Georgia. She embraced her experiences in the internship and was soon promoted as a leader!

Dictionary.com defines internship as "an official or formal program to provide practical experiences for beginners in an occupation or profession." When choosing a career, it is imperative that you know what you have committed to do from day to day. Being an educator is the only career I have ever considered. The internship experience as an administrator in a school building was an eye-opening experience that better prepared me to take on the role of assistant principal. The experiences in my internship directly related to managing the organization, the daily operation of the school, the allocation of resources within the school, and the promotion of an effective school environment.

School leaders have the task of managing the school environment while meeting the demands placed on the school by school board officials. The school leader essentially serves the role of the "middle-man" in producing the product of student achievement because they don't directly instruct students and don't draft the mandates or required goals at each individual school. He or she is bringing order and structure on both ends and assists with making an individualized plan for his or her school.

As a classroom teacher, you often think to yourself, *I'm very capable of being an administrator,* because you don't realize the stress of the position. The administrator's position almost seems glamorous because they are always well dressed, they get to leave during the day, are allowed to arrive later in the day, attend meetings with other adults, and give you directives on what needs to happen without knowing that your classes are "unique." These are perceived myths from the faculty and staff in the school building due to the position resembling the miners saying, "Everything that glitters isn't gold."

While the position of an administrator is held in high esteem, it comes with long hours and deadlines like any other job in the education profession. Principals have to dress professionally because appearance is sometimes everything. They represent the school to the community, and every parent wants to believe they are sending their child to a quality institution that is run by a professional.

The meetings that administrators attend during the day aren't so glamorous either. The meetings may sometimes be redundant in nature or present a new goal for the school to accomplish on top of the other twenty goals at hand. The meetings may or may not be scheduled in advance, which can create a problem when you are trying to manage the inside of the school from the outside. They often discuss with school board officials the progress of the other goals and are assured this goal is similar to the work that the school is already doing. The administrator tries to do what they can at the district level, prior to giving directives to the teachers, which may tip their scale of work and make them disgruntled.

After completing an internship and knowing the work that is involved, why would someone want to work in that field? I hope that the answer to this question is similar to my belief that as an administrator I: serve as an academic advocate for students, an instructional leader for teachers, and an education ambassador to the community. The internship experience was very beneficial in preparing me to be a future leader by allowing me to assist my principal in problem solving without the direct responsibility. When similar problems arise, my prior knowledge allows me to create an effective solution. Learning to "put out fires quickly" by addressing the problem and developing a plan was the most beneficial skill acquired during the experience.

Due to the value of my experience, I often reflect and express my gratitude to my internship mentor and professors. Unfortunately, I learned the lesson that red tape isn't as easy to cut away as it appears, but it's easier to navigate around it to achieve your goal. I believe I have grown in the areas of instructional and visionary leadership because I understand the value of a shared vision among leaders and their staff, and the impact leadership vision has on the instructional practices within their school. Cultural leadership is an area of growth that I am working on by setting the tone of acceptance and appreciation as my current principal does, and not allowing the outside influences dictate the internal environment.

Having a working knowledge of each area of leadership has assisted me in becoming a dynamic leader. When serving as a transformational leader, it is imperative to lead in a manner that reflects integrity and fairness as an important part of the work we do. My ability to act with integrity will influence the students, teachers and community as a whole because stakeholder's value and respect your input. The education that is provided within the school you lead largely impacts the world outside of the school as well as the future of the community. Hearing from each stakeholder and their position on education provides another point of view for consideration when making decisions that will drive instruction and impact student achievement.

The importance of establishing a true learning community where individuals can express their thoughts and have those thoughts taken into account are necessary to the success of the school. While I have not anticipated every occurrence, during my internship I learned to have a plan to guide me in my thought processes and help me to develop a plan of action; this has greatly helped in my current role. Our administrative team works as a team to manage the school environment. Our common theme proves to be successful in increasing the academic achievement of students and the quality of the education that is provided, even in a high-achieving school. With adequate monitoring of the practices of the instructional program and school environment, leaders will be effective managers.

While I believe being an educator is a calling, being an effective leader is a learning process that is nurtured through internship opportunities and quality leaders whose shared experience shape you into becoming an effective leader.

ANDRIA YOUNG BUNNER

Andria is a leader who is always "hungry" for knowledge and learning! Today she owns a consulting business and has served many districts throughout the state. She continues to grow and learn and is always open to challenges in her leadership journey!

The mentoring aspect of Educational Leadership began for me during my summer intern experience. It was three weeks of unpaid work, bus duty, dealing with discipline, and helping to administer the retest for students who had failed the state assessment in May. This adventure sounded like the perfect way to spend my summer vacation. The reality of the situation was dreadful. Just thinking about giving up the three weeks of my summer made me completely frustrated.

Prior to summer school starting, I met for a planning session with the principal who would serve as my mentor for the three-week experience. We talked about schedules for classes, buses, dealing with discipline and other responsibilities for our time together. The meeting went well. I really liked the individual who would serve as my mentor. I started to think that maybe I could actually handle the experience.

The first day of summer school arrived. The usual problems that come with the first day were evident: students not knowing their bus number, students in the wrong classes, and a few who just were not registered. These challenges were met by the administrator with an incredible amount of professionalism. I watched how each student, regardless of the situation, was treated with an incredible amount of respect. I also observed how irate parents never frazzled the administrator in charge.

Dismissal also came with its own unique challenges. A few children did not get on the correct bus, others were returned because an adult was not home, or they simply waited in the car-rider line when they needed to be on the bus. Once again, the administrator in charge did not let any of this bother her. Two hours after dismissal, all students had finally left the building.

My nerves were completely shot. A pounding headache

prevented me from thinking clearly. Surely this was not going to be the typical way summer school would take place. Did I really have to return to do this again? Why am I really here?

The administrator in charge met with those of us who were serving on her administrative team after all the children had been dismissed. She informed us that this had been a really great first day. All I could think was how glad I was it was over. I was also informed I needed to take a more active role. The question was posed, "How about taking over the arrival and dismissal of the buses?" How can one say "no"?

The rest of the week went much smoother. I managed very humid mornings greeting the students as they stepped off the bus. During the week, many of the students would not say anything as they were getting off the bus. I tried to learn all their names and speak to each student. I also began to learn the names of all the summer school faculty members.

Each day, the leadership program I was involved in required a reflection of the day and week. I can remember writing, "I survived," followed by, "I do not know how this principal handles so many high stress situations." I thought about those thoughts for the rest of the evening. I hoped the following days would not bring pounding headaches and parents who were unhappy. I also realized I had learned my first real lesson about real leadership.

Lesson Learned

Leadership requires an individual to not show stress, and to remember, no matter how difficult the situation, to treat everyone involved with respect.

The summer progressed with many opportunities for discipline, being engaged with the curriculum, and various issues that traditionally face any summer school program. The mentor working with me knew I was very "green." By the beginning of summer school, I had only completed a very small portion of my educational leadership classes. Not only was I "green," but very overwhelmed. I truly believe the greatest thing that happened to me over the course of summer school was being able to watch my mentor handle situations. Once it was my turn to handle a similar situation, I never had to guess how my mentor would want me to handle it.

LESSON LEARNED

Leaders lead by example. Good leadership requires a leader to model, model, and model again the expectations they have for a building.

After finishing my summer experience, I enjoyed a few days of rest, relaxation, and some quiet time. I began to reflect on the summer lessons I had learned. I pondered my last conversation with my summer mentor. We had gone over all the paper requirements to be returned to the college for my credits. One of the sheets to be completed was a discussion session about the summer. I had to highlight points where I learned valuable lessons. I shared how I appreciated how her leadership style was truly by example. I also appreciated how she sacrificed many hours for the summer school program. This great leader was not leaving once the clock said it was time to leave.

Many observations occurred involving how she had made arrangements for her family to continue with the summer events such as basketball camp, travel, sports practice, along with other family obligations. My mentor asked me which area I thought would be considered a strength—discipline or curriculum. Of course, I had no hesitation. Curriculum, by far, was viewed as my strength. This insightful lady challenged me to use the remaining portion of my Educational Leadership program to work on perfecting my strengths and developing my weaknesses into areas of growth. We talked about her personal journey in leadership, and how she was able to focus and develop her strengths and work on her weaknesses. This was more than likely the most powerful part of my summer. I just did not realize how, at the time, it would impact my future.

Lesson Learned

Great leaders know their own strengths and weaknesses.

The fall session of Educational Leadership classes started back with the announcement of one hundred and twenty hours of shadowing with a new mentor. My first reaction was, how in the world I would be able to fit these hours into my schedule? I also had to find a leader in my building to agree to become my mentor. My principal suggested the new assistant principal. The assistant principal had just been assigned to the school. Upon our first meeting, my new mentor told me she had just one rule—I had to be honest with her, and she would be honest with me. The fortunate aspect of my job during this time was that I was serving as a reading teacher assigned to different classrooms. I found creative times (such as when classes were away for a field trip or having a guest speaker) to schedule opportunities to engage in hands-on activities with my mentor. I sacrificed at least one planning session a week and worked during many lunch breaks.

Once we had truly established the trust factor between the two of us, I began to have opportunities I never imagined would take place. I was presented certain scenarios regarding discipline, parents, curriculum, and other leadership issues. My mentor would ask me to explain how I would handle the issue. We would talk about my answer and why or why not this would be a good response. From the beginning, my mentor picked up that discipline was not a strong point for me. The parent component and curriculum scenarios tended to be stronger but needed some polishing. I truly believe that because we had established the honesty guidelines from the beginning, I did not take any of the feedback personally or in an attacking manner. Trust me, some of the feedback I received was not pretty, but it helped me to grow into the person I am today. My new mentor would be so honest with me. She never tried to tiptoe around how I needed to grow, but gave suggestions how to make my answers to the different scenarios better. I also had the opportunity to observe how this honesty was not just with me, but with other adults and students. Many years have passed, and I realize the value of not being rude, but tactfully honest with those in the education profession. The bottom line is that everything that takes place in a building ultimately impacts the life of a child, and what adults are doing needs to be done correctly.

LESSON LEARNED

Honesty must be part of the leadership skills used daily—no dancing around, just straight up honesty from the heart, with passion and conviction. A leader must realize that honesty is often hard to share, but must be backed up with solutions of how to help the individual grow and improve. Feedback is a powerful tool between a mentee and mentor. Verbal feedback is a powerful for our students, but it must be handled in a supportive and constructive, professional manner.

The course of the year continued, and I had more than the required 120-shadowing hours completed well before the due date. There were many opportunities to attend county meetings, help with school ceremonies to recognize students, help plan parent events, assist with presentations, and observe in classrooms. I can honestly say that until I observed all of these activities with my mentor, I looked at life with a different set of eyes. My conception of how daily activities run for a school leader was truly different from what I observed. Until this point, my view of school leadership had only been from the confines of the four walls of my classroom or the portable cart I had been assigned. Many times, I found myself observing situations where I wondered how my mentor was able to keep her cool. Dreams would have never begun to adequately describe situations that I never knew happened on a daily basis.

Looking back, these are just NORMAL, everyday occurrences that take place in a building (school fights, upset parents, upset teachers, buses late or not showing up, and multiple discipline issues, not to mention curriculum issues). Many times, my mentor would ask me how to handle a situation. My response sometimes was, "You have got to be kidding. This really did not happen." Often my mentor would smile and tell me to listen and learn. Toward the end of our mentoring relationship, the comment changed to "Come with me; it's time for you to now watch and learn." This statement often meant she was locating me at various times to go on what I liked to call a "quick observational field trip."

I became accustomed to discipline and learned not to be shocked by what was taking place each day. I also became accustomed to parents and observed how to help handle these individuals. This experience allowed me to see what is considered normal in the life of a school administrator and very different in the eyes of a classroom teacher. I believe many times we all take for granted what truly goes on each day to run a school. Teachers become consumed with their responsibilities and fail to realize that it is an administrator's full-time job to run a school correctly.

LESSON LEARNED

During each situation, I saw one specific aspect of how my mentor handled herself. Calmness always prevailed, along with consistency. Many times, I observed the same issue with the same child. Her behavior and reaction always displayed a sense of calm. She knew when to use what I like to refer to as a firm voice—never yelling, but changing the tone enough to make a vital point become very clear. Consistency as a leader is crucial to the culture of the building. Parents, students, and teachers are watching how a leader reacts.

Here's a question to think about as a future leader:

What level of professionalism will you display daily?

During the time of calculating hours toward my Educational Leadership Specialist degree, I found myself presented with tasks that made me uncomfortable. Why? Because these situations were out of my comfort zone. I was asked to conduct the honor roll ceremony, which was held each nine weeks. I had to present, at a faculty meeting, about data the school was using to drive our instruction for teaching Reading. These two uncomfortable situations mentioned are only a few of the ones I found myself facing. I realize now my mentor was asking me to conduct these different situations not because she wanted to, but because I was comfortable talking with children, not adults. Before my very first faculty presentation, my mentor found me in the restroom looking like I was about to pass out. All I remember is her telling me to drink water and that I had to go and do the presentation. She said she would be in the front row if I needed her. Once I opened my mouth and started talking, everything turned out to be all right. I survived and did not pass out (much to my mentor's surprise, I'm sure).

Lesson Learned

A good mentor will push a mentee in order to help the individual grow. Being uncomfortable will truly make a person grow. A great mentor will always be there for support and encouragement, which shows signs of also being a strong leader.

I also learned that school leaders are often more than just the leaders of a building. I saw firsthand how a school leader is often the first to find out about death, terminal illnesses, home life problems, and general day-to-day concerns from staff members, all things that have nothing to do with what is taking place inside the building. The saying is true—people do bring their problems to work. I was not privileged to the private conversations. What I was privileged to witness was giving hugs, eyes that looked as if they had been filled with tears, and knowing the expressions on staff members faces to know when to stop everything and just listen. What I also observed is how my mentor built relationships. Each morning she went to every classroom to greet each teacher.

LESSON LEARNED

A good administrator will push themselves to get to know the entire staff, read their facial expressions, and be able to understand body language. They establish relationships and are always genuine. They are never fake or insincere.

Life After My Experience of Having a Mentor

I moved from years of teaching in the classroom to being a Title I reading teacher. I then became a building instructional coach, then later serve at the district level in the same capacity. Life led me to the State Department of Education, and later to opening my own consulting company. I reflect back on my times with my mentor and realize I learned far more about leadership than I realized while taking notes and completing class work. I also realized a mentor would always be there for me. Since leaving my original mentors, I have developed a few others along the way whom I call for curriculum questions and business advice. These individuals are invaluable. They help me to grow, push me to new professional levels, and keep me accountable.

Following are a few lessons I've learned about leadership that I did not learn from a mentor, but, I believe they are vital to anyone who will mentor or practice leadership in your building. I call these "Lessons from the Field":

- Not everyone will share the same educational philosophy that you share. You need to stand your ground and be ready to defend the reasons you believe what you believe.

- Realize why you went into education—is it for the paycheck or the students?

- You are going to be watched every step of the way. Make sure you can defend your actions at all times. If you are going to end up on the front page of the local paper, make sure it is for a reason you are proud to defend, not because you were acting out of character.

- Always dress for success. Each day, regardless of what you are doing, you are on an interview. Make sure you are dressing for your next job, even if you are not looking for another job. One individual you will come in contact with will need to write a recommendation letter. Always think about what they will write. There may be a question they are asked about professional dress.

- Stay true to yourself and what you believe. Never change because it is popular for the situation.

- Always stay up-to-date with educational issues. We live in an ever-changing world, and you never want to be the last to know about a current event in education.

- Never forget where you came from. We all started as teachers. These individuals are the most important people impacting the lives of our students. Always be willing to listen, help, and offer suggestions.

- Never ask your staff or the group you are working with to do a task you are not willing to do yourself. Individuals respect you once they see you are willing to get "down and dirty."

- There is a media advertisement that states "Kindness Works, Pass It On." These are powerful words for all of us to consider. I am thankful for the unconditional kindness my mentors have always displayed to me. We need to make sure we do this with all we come in contact with each day.

I consider my time working on my leadership certification a valuable experience. I am grateful for the time I spent with those who have served as my official mentors. You have taught me about life as a leader, but most importantly, you helped me to grow into the individual I am today. A special thanks to Gerri Hawkins, Alison Jackson, and Dr. Mary Jacobs. You are three ladies who really were able to see me come out of my shell. Thank you!

CHAPTER 7
CELEBRATIONS AND LESSONS FROM PERFORMANCE COACHES

─────────────────────────

&

"Be a yardstick of quality. Some people aren't used to an environment where excellence is expected."

— Steve Jobs

&

I HAVE ALWAYS BELIEVED that hiring the best and the brightest and allowing them to do their work is powerful! The same is true when you are associated with outstanding mentors. I posed questions to the mentors I work with to gather and assist with future mentors and their journeys.

QUESTION 1

How long have you been involved in coaching and mentoring potential leaders?

Cindy:

After my retirement five years ago, I began working formally with mentees. However, as a twenty-seven year veteran principal, I had many leaders I mentored. I feel strongly that it is imperative to give back to the profession! I have enjoyed mentoring for a number of reasons. The main ones include: always learning from the students; keeping abreast of new initiatives and trends in the state; and continuing to be realistic about the administrator's duties and responsibilities.

Vic:

Once I retired (and failed my retirement), I began to explore a passion and perhaps even a calling. After more than thirty years in leadership roles that ranged from principal to central office and even a human resource director for one of the largest districts in the state, I returned to the Department of Education and served as a director for a leadership program for leaders in the state. The program was called Leadership 21. A large part of the program was to assign trained mentors to the aspiring leaders. During this time, I saw the value of a person having a trained mentor. We talked about this a great deal, but to see how it worked was amazing. I have continued to seek and train mentors to assist leaders.

QUESTION 2

What powerful lessons have you learned along the way?

Cindy:

There are so many things I have learned, but the power of relationships with students, parents and administrators and, of course, the community, is vital to being an effective leader. Another lesson learned is that enthusiasm is contagious! Honesty and integrity will stand behind your beliefs and will endure the test of time. Also, say what you mean and mean what you say! And perhaps a golden rule I try to live by is: "Treat every day as a gift."

Vic:

The selection process for a mentor is a key element. You must find folks who are willing to give the time and have a passion for the work. Mentors must have the ability to listen. If you really think about listening, you will find this is difficult for some of us. Communication skills are a key element. This includes written and oral communication. The ability to establish a positive and honest relationship is a must, along with having enthusiasm for life.

QUESTION 3

What is the most challenging part of mentoring?

Cindy:

- Having people open up and admitting when things are difficult.

- Building trust and relationships.

- Focusing on the problems and coaching, then to solve the problem, not giving them the answer.

Vic:

- Giving the time and attention to the work.

- Allowing candidates time to focus on matters of concern.

- Building a positive relationship.

QUESTION 4

Explain the changes you have observed during the last ten years.

Cindy:

- Commitment to job.

- Work ethic.

- Not knowing how to build relationships.

- Integrity.

Vic:

- Arranging time to be an effective coach/mentor.

- Having the value of mentors understood by school leaders.

- Having those who serve as mentors being recognized by their leaders.

Question 5:

Is there a success story that you remember? If so, please explain.

Vic:

I recommended a recent graduate for a position as a high school science teacher. Five years later, I was asked by a local superintendent to recommend a person for assistant principal in a middle school. This person was hired, and after three years, he called me to talk about applying for a principal position. We spent some sessions getting prepared for the interview. He secured the position, and three years later was hired by one of the largest high schools in Georgia, then became area superintendent in the largest school system in the state. This person took advantage of his experiences and was committed to always learning.

CHAPTER 8
EVALUATIONS

"True genius resides in the capacity for evaluation of uncertain hazardous, and conflicting information..."

— Winston Churchill

W HEN YOU THINK of evaluations, it is not in the sense of right or wrong, but continuous improvement. This is a notion that has changed throughout the years in some arenas.

When we address how to evaluate the process appropriately, we think of several different levels. The first area of evaluation comes with the candidate being ready for the internship. They must have enough experience to not only observe and participate, but also lead!

The best way to do this is to ask the candidate, coach, and the local supporting mentor. Once this is determined, then you will know how to move forward and address any issues you may have discovered.

The next level of evaluation comes with the internship experience. You need to determine any areas that were not fully explained or understood. It is always important to find the right folks to coach and mentor others. When a situation appears where the candidate is having difficulty during the internship, it is imperative the coach step in and address the problem. Many times, it is a lack of time that has been devoted by the locally based sponsor or mentor.

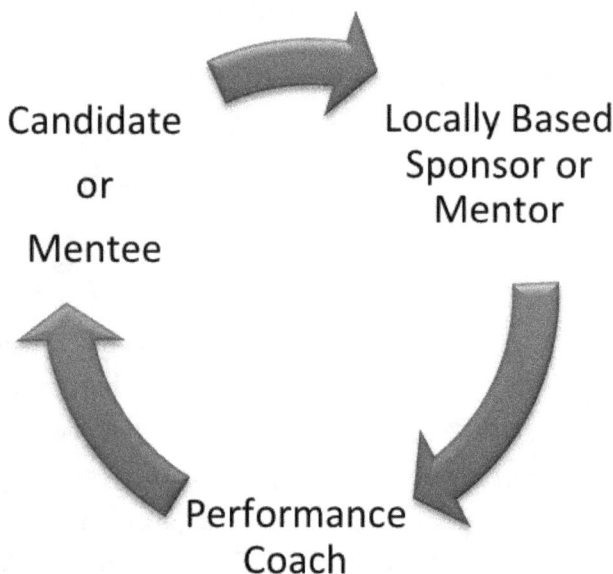

The third point to evaluate is the experience from the mentee's perspective. Ask them about the strengths and the weaknesses of the experience, and whether they have any suggestions for continuous improvement. When there is strong trust among the stakeholders, it is amazing how honest and open they will be with you.

The final point to evaluate is the area of the goals of the candidates. You need to note the goals and correlate them to the ISLLC standards to help determine any specific needs that may be addressed prior to the yearlong internship. Many times, you will find that some of the standards overlap each other. By doing this, the candidate is assured when they go to the next interview that they are well equipped to answer the question, "What is your area of weakness?" The response will be, "It was such and such, but due to my internship experience, this is how that has been improved." What a powerful statement!

REFLECTION:

Think of the last time you were evaluated. Was there something you should have mentioned but didn't?

_____

_____

_____

_____

How do you typically respond to evaluations and constructive criticism? If a mentee makes suggestions for improvements, how would you respond? Would you be hurt, angry, or happy? Think about different responses you might have and think of how you can embrace all of the critiques you receive.

_____

_____

CHAPTER 9

PAYING IT FORWARD

❧

*"Even if I knew tomorrow the world would go to pieces,
I would still plant my apple tree."*

— Martin Luther

❧

I ONCE WAS ASKED how I wished to be remembered. This is a powerful question, because it makes you realize your core values. For me, these can be put in several categories. The overarching theme is "making a difference," not only in my professional life and career, but my personal life as well. That is why the concept of *paying it forward*, has become an important one in my life.

Think about the balance of your life…what happens when you get off balance? You have to maintain your focus. When you only pay attention and build one part of your life then other parts will not be as strong.

It always amazes me that the news makes such a big fuss over a person doing the right things and paying it forward. Should this not be our daily life and mindset? I think it should be! Let's explore how this can work for us if you ONLY pay attention! Look at the diagram below and ask yourself: What will my legacy be?

Emotional and Spiritual Balance

Think about your belief systems and your spiritual well-being. If you do not have a loving spirit and spiritual nature then you are missing a great deal of joy from your life. Remember the old saying about identifying as an optimist or pessimist? Is your glass half full or is it half empty? I am not asking you to be a "Pollyanna," but you can make what you wish of your day. If you get up in the morning and only fill your life with negative thoughts, that is probably what you will get each day. Try to replace each negative thought with a positive one.

What are you doing to build this part of your life? You must do this in order to be there for the others that you wish to help. You must feed your own spirit and emotional behavior. Ways that I have learned to do this are reading, praying, and thinking of others on a daily basis. What brings you calmness in your day?

REFLECTION:

Name three things that bring calmness to you

1. _____
2. _____
3. _____

Share your list and then revisit it in a few months to see if it has changed.

Woman's Club Story

About four years ago, my mother passed away after a lengthy illness. In the end, she was wheelchair bound and had to be on oxygen all the time. After she passed away, I knew I had to do something that would re-spark and invent my emotional and spiritual well-being. First, I decided it would be food, but after about twelve pounds, I realized that was only temporary solution; so I decided I would read, pray and think more about life.

Along the way, I decided to join the woman's club in our area. The ladies all had a purpose and wanted to serve and give back to the community. All of a sudden, I was asked to be the president of the club. That was not part of my plan, but as I looked around at the members I thought, *These ladies have done a lot for the community, and they are in their seventies, eighties, and one lady is ninety-five!* I needed to practice what I often preach about giving back to others. I must say it has been delightful in the last two years of service. We have focused on building the club, having fun, fundraising for scholarships, food banks and needy families. What a pleasure to give back in a small way to bring joy to others and to yourself. Oh, by the way, I am one of the younger ones in the group. The reason I mention that is one day it will be another person's turn, and they will be saying the same thing! What a difference it would make if we all gave to others just four to five hours a month.

Elderly Lady in the Dollar Store

Yes, I frequent dollar stores on a regular basis! Recently I was in a dollar store and the lady in front of me was purchasing some canned meat items. The items were probably about three or four dollars and she was using a gift card to make the purchase. The clerk told her that she did not have any funds left on the card. The elderly lady dropped her head and began to leave. I quietly told the clerk that I would pay for it. She turned and said, "Thank you."

After she left, I thought I should have done more for her. When I left the store, she was gone. But, it reminded me that we need to notice our surroundings more. There are so many more elderly and needy people whose day we can make a bit brighter. This takes skills of observation and practice, but remember: It is the small things in life that will bring you joy!

REFLECTION:

These are just a few examples of how I've been able to pay it forward. Have you ever experienced the kindness of a stranger? Or have you ever paid it forward in a meaningful way?

_____

_____

_____

_____

_____

Jack's Story

Several years ago my brother, Jack, died. He had been in a couple of serious car accidents and even was knocked out in one. After the accidents, he began to change. He was not well, and we knew this due to his behavior. I had tried several times to call and check on him, but failed each time. On a Wednesday night, I was speaking with my youngest brother by phone, and we were discussing Jack. I shared with my brother that I had tried to reach him several times, but was unable to connect. He suggested that when we finished our conversation I try and call him again. I told him that I would.

I will always remember that Wednesday night when at nine o'clock I dialed my brother's number ONE more time. To my amazement he answered the phone. We talked about our families and just light chit-chat. As we ended the conversation, we told each other we loved each other. We didn't often do that.

My brother, Jack, committed suicide on the following Saturday at 4:15.

As I write this, I can still feel the last time we spoke. He was only fifty-seven years old. After his death, I vowed that each and every day of my life I would reach out to a friend or family member just to check on them. Sometimes I have to leave a voice message, but that just lets them know someone cares.

How will you show someone in your life that you care?

_____

_____

_____

_____

_____

_____

Final Thoughts

I hope you can use this book to help you find joy in your life as well as bring joy to others.

Some of the best days of my life are when I hear from a former student, at either the elementary level or the university level, and they share their successes! Wow, what a powerful day that is for me. Many of my students will contact me when they have experienced a positive event in their lives, or even when they have questions and wish to have honest, open feedback for a situation.

Last words to remember: It has been an honor and a privilege to serve as an educator and life-long coach and mentor for other educators, and especially leaders for the future.

Take a few moments to think about your legacy and how you wish to be remembered:

_____

_____

_____

_____

_____

_____

_____

_____

_____

_____

_____

_____

_____

_____

_____

_____

_____

_____

_____

_____

NOTES FOR THE FUTURE

It is imperative to continue to grow and be reflective!

Revisit this book after a year and write down your reflections.

Year 1:

What have you learned?

_____

_____

_____

What else do you wish to learn?

_____

_____

_____

Describe a challenging situation. What did you do?

_____

_____

_____

_____

Are you seeing any common themes? If, so what are they?

_____

_____

_____

Year 2:

What have you learned?

_____

_____

_____

What else do you wish to learn?

_____

_____

_____

_____

Describe a challenging situation. What did you do?

_____

_____

_____

_____

Are you seeing any common themes? If, so what are they?

_____

_____

_____

Year 5:

What have you learned?

_____

_____

_____

What else do you wish to learn?

_____

_____

_____

_____

Describe a challenging situation. What did you do?

_____

_____

_____

_____

Are you seeing any common themes? If, so what are they?

_____

_____

_____

Year 10:

What have you learned?

_____

_____

_____

_____

What else do you wish to learn?

_____

_____

_____

_____

Describe a challenging situation. What did you do?

_____

_____

_____

_____

Are you seeing any common themes? If, so what are they?

_____

_____

_____

_____

COACHING RESOURCES

Coach Training Alliance, Boulder, CO. Home courses and online programs: http://www.coachtrainingalliance.com/

Academy of Creative Coaching, Atlanta, GA. In-person or online programs: http://academyofcreativecoaching.com/

ABOUT THE AUTHOR

Dr. Mary Jacobs

As Coordinator of the EdS Program and Internships at Mercer University, Dr. Mary Jacobs has proved she has a passion for educating children, adults, and improving schools across Georgia. She serves as a consultant for various school systems, as well.

Dr. Jacobs was appointed to Coordinator of the EdS Program in 2009. Prior to this position, she served as the Curriculum Director in Butts County where she lead the SACS district accreditation for five schools in the area, focused on overall school improvement, and offered counsel to educators on data-driven discussions.

Prior to her current role, Dr. Jacobs was Principal at Henderson Middle School (HMS) in Jackson, Georgia for seven years. While at HMS, she drove improvement of school attendance from over 40 percent of students missing 15 or more days, down to 12 percent. Test scores also showed improvement year after year under her leadership.

Before joining HMS, Dr. Jacobs served as Assistant Principal for schools in Butts and Gwinnett counties, combining more than six years of AP tenure at the elementary education level. These school sizes ranged from 600 to 1,200 students.

Dr. Jacobs also served as an adjunct professor for ten years at Mercer University in Georgia teaching assessment, curriculum and school improvement classes, as well as serving on the advisory board for their PhD program.

Earning a bachelor's degree in Early Childhood from the University of Georgia, a master's degree from Georgia Southwestern, and a doctorate degree from Nova University in Educational Leadership, Jacobs' has a proven and solid track record in not only educating herself, but in communicating the value of educating others.

In the past thirty plus years, Dr. Jacobs has served in many facets of education ranging from school administration to college-level, private consulting, to serving in the classroom. She has also contributed to *Middle Grounds,* and has been quoted in many newspapers including *The Atlanta-Journal Constitution* and *Jackson Progress-Argus.*

Dr. Jacobs was born in Washington, Georgia, and currently resides in Monticello, Georgia, with her husband. She has two children and three grandchildren.